Conten

Dinosaur World

Have you ever been to a wildlife park?
Have you ever seen lions, zebras, camels
or chimps from a bus or car? You can
get very near the animals and watch
them washing, feeding and playing.

Imagine you could visit a wildlife park called Dinosaur World. This park has dinosaurs and other animals from the distant past. It has a tour bus for you to ride around the park. So hop on the bus and enjoy a trip round Dinosaur World!

A map of the park

Most of the animals in Dinosaur World lived in the Jurassic and Cretaceous **eras**. Take a look at this map of the park and you will see where all the dinosaurs are and where the bus will stop.

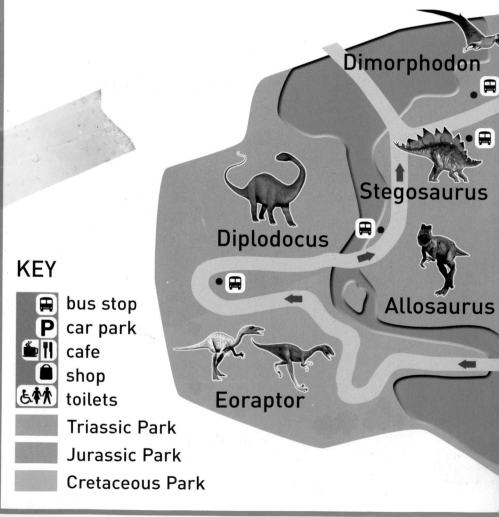

Dimorphodon

Stegosaurus

Diplodocus

Allosaurus

Eoraptor

KEY

🚌	bus stop
P	car park
☕🍴	cafe
🛍	shop
♿🚻	toilets
	Triassic Park
	Jurassic Park
	Cretaceous Park

When the bus stops in Jurassic Park you will see dinosaurs that lived between 200 and 145 million years ago. The bus tour ends in Cretaceous Park. Here you can see dinosaurs that lived between 145 and 65 million years ago.

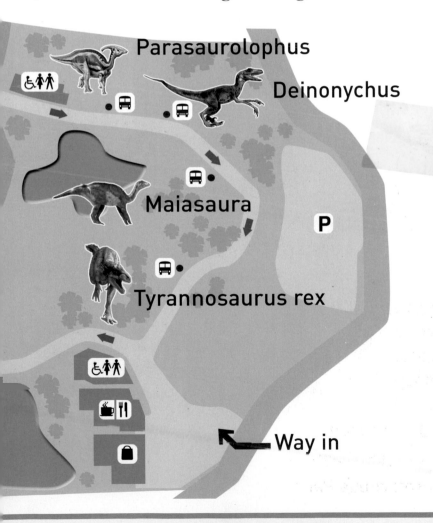

Parasaurolophus

Deinonychus

Maiasaura

P

Tyrannosaurus rex

Way in

What are dinosaurs?

Dinosaurs are animals that lived on Earth a very long time ago. They lived between about 250 and 65 million years ago and they were the most important land animals of their time. This long stretch of Earth's history is split into three parts, the Triassic, the Jurassic and the Cretaceous eras.

Triassic era
251–200 million years ago

Jurassic era
200–145 million years ago

Cretaceous era
145–65 million years ago

Eoraptor

Dinosaurs led different sorts of lives. Many of them ate plants such as **conifers** and **ferns**. Other dinosaurs ate meat and were the deadliest hunters the world has ever seen.

Dinosaurs come in many shapes and sizes.

Diplodocus

Deinonychus

Stegosaurus

Diplodocus

When the bus stops, the first dinosaurs you see are a herd of Diplodocus. A Diplodocus has a big body, strong legs, a long neck, a small head and a long tail. It is huge!

Diplodocus feed on bushes and trees, tearing off the leaves with their teeth. Plants are tough, so the Diplodocus swallow stones which help to crush the food in their stomach. Animals this big eat all the time just to stay alive.

Diplodocus has teeth like this.

Ferns are food for Diplodocus and other plant-eaters.

Fact sheet: Diplodocus
Size: up to 35 metres long
Habitat: near rivers
Food: moss, ferns and trees
Lived: 155–145 million years ago

Danger rating: ★ ☆ ☆

Allosaurus

The next dinosaur in Dinosaur World is a big beast called Allosaurus. It eats meat, and is one of the deadliest killers of its time. What makes it such a good hunter?

Allosaurus can spot animals that are sick or weak. It can stand on its strong back legs and run very fast. It has big jaws, sharp teeth and long claws to strip the meat from its **prey**.

Fact sheet: Allosaurus
Size: up to 9 metres long
Habitat: grasslands and forest
Food: other dinosaurs
Lived: 155–144 million years ago

Danger rating: ★ ★ ★

Stegosaurus

Next we visit a dinosaur called
Stegosaurus. It is about the same size
as Allosaurus, but it walks on four legs.
It has bony **studs** to protect its neck, hard
plates along its back and **spines** on its tail.

Stegosaurus eats plants, so it does not need sharp teeth or claws. If a meat-eater attacks, Stegosaurus swings its tail and smashes the hunter with its spines!

Stegosaurus has sharp spines on its tail.

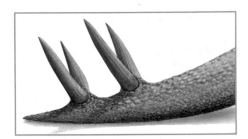

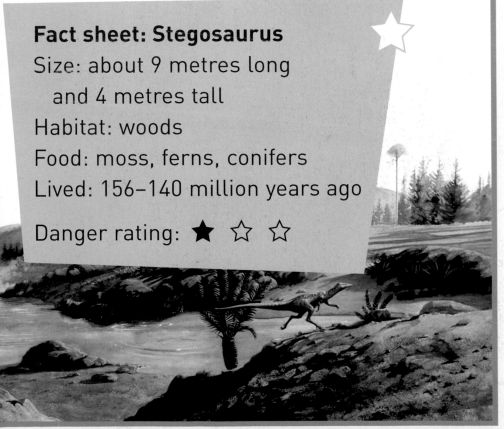

Fact sheet: Stegosaurus
Size: about 9 metres long
    and 4 metres tall
Habitat: woods
Food: moss, ferns, conifers
Lived: 156–140 million years ago

Danger rating: ★ ☆ ☆

Dimorphodon

There are animals flying around the park called **pterosaurs**. They are related to dinosaurs and at first they look a bit like birds.

Then you see one close up. It is called Dimorphodon and it is not like a bird at all!

Dimorphodon has jaws that are full of teeth and its wings are made of skin, not feathers. In one way Dimorphodon *is* like a bird. It catches insects in its mouth as it flies through the air.

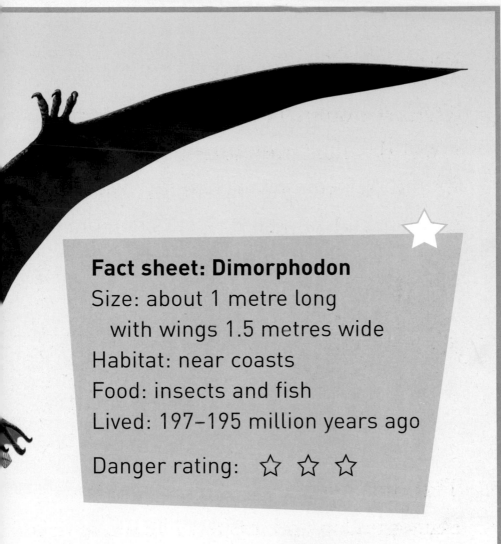

Fact sheet: Dimorphodon

Size: about 1 metre long
   with wings 1.5 metres wide
Habitat: near coasts
Food: insects and fish
Lived: 197–195 million years ago

Danger rating: ☆ ☆ ☆

Dimorphodon
has lots of
sharp teeth
in its jaws.

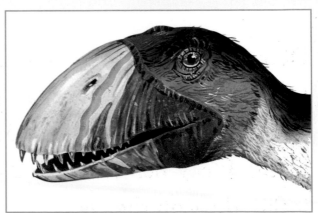

Duckbill dinosaurs

Now the bus is going to visit dinosaurs from the Cretaceous era, more than 65 million years ago. There are herds of dinosaurs feeding by a river. They are called duckbill dinosaurs.

Parasaurolophus

Each herd has a different crest on their head and a different skin pattern too. A duckbill called Parasaurolophus calls to its herd. It makes a loud booming sound. Not all duckbills boom – some honk or squeak.

Crests come in different colours and shapes.

Fact sheet: Parasaurolophus

Size: about 10 metres long

Habitat: rivers, lakes and coasts

Food: pine needles, leaves, twigs and ferns

Lived: 76–65 million years ago

Danger rating: ★ ☆ ☆

Deinonychus

Deinonychus is the size of a small car,
has long, slim legs and runs very fast.
It has 60 curving teeth and claws on its
hands and feet. One claw on each foot is
long and curved to cut and slash its prey.

Deinonychus is not just speedy, it is smart,
too. These animals eat anything and
hunt in **packs**. Together, they
kill big duckbills and
other plant-eating
dinosaurs.

Fact sheet: Deinonychus
Size: up to 3 metres long
Habitat: swamps and forests
Food: meat
Lived: 115–108 million years ago

Danger rating: ★ ★ ★

The curved claw is
13 centimetres long!

A pack of Deinonychus
attack a big
plant-eater.

Maiasaura

A herd of duckbill dinosaurs called Maiasaura have made their nests in the sand by a lake. Can you see a sneaky little dinosaur called Chirostenotes grabbing one of the eggs in its jaws?

Baby Maiasaura are very small when they hatch. When they get bigger and can walk, the herd leaves the beach to look for food. They will return to nest next year.

A Maiasaura egg

Fact sheet: Maiasaura
Size: about 9 metres long
Habitat: by rivers and lakes
Food: leaves, berries, seeds, ferns and conifers
Lived: 80–65 million years ago

Danger rating (nesting): ★ ★ ★

Tyrannosaurus rex

Tyrannosaurus rex is one of the biggest hunters of the Cretaceous era. Its massive head has strong jaws that can crush bone.

Tyrannosaurus rex hunts alone. It creeps very near to a plant-eater, then charges on its strong back legs. It grabs the animal in its jaws, then bites it with its teeth. Its teeth are as long and sharp as daggers. If they break, new ones grow in their place.

Fact sheet: Tyrannosaurus rex
Size: about 12 metres long
Habitat: warm forests, near
    rivers and swamps
Food: meat
Lived: 85–65 million years ago

Danger rating: ★ ★ ★

Some Tyrannosaurus teeth are 30 centimetres long.

Clues about dinosaurs

Our trip around Dinosaur World is over. There is no such place in the real world because dinosaurs became **extinct** about 65 million years ago. We can still find out about them by looking at clues hidden in rocks. These clues are called **fossils**.

These people are digging out the fossils of dinosaur bones.

How a fossil is made

A dinosaur dies by a river. Sand and mud cover it.

Over millions of years, the sand and mud change into rock. The bones become fossils.

The rock is worn away by wind and water. When the fossils are found, an expert digs them up.

A dinosaur museum

Many dinosaur fossils end up in museums. When experts have a lot of bones, they try to make a skeleton. The skeleton shows the size of an animal, what it looked like and what it ate. It does not show what colour it was or what sounds it made.

A Tyrannosaurus rex skeleton in the American Museum of Natural History

Other fossils add to the story. Footprints show how an animal stood and moved. They show if it lived alone or with others in a herd. People are finding new fossils all the time. They help us to learn about the dinosaur world.

A fossilized dinosaur footprint

You can see the bony plates along the back of this Stegosaurus skeleton.

Glossary

conifer A tree that grows cones, such as a pine tree.

era A period of time in the past.

extinct No longer living on the Earth.

fern A green plant that has no flowers.

fossil A part of an animal that has turned to stone.

pack A group of animals that hunt together.

plate A hard, flat bit of horn or bone that protects an animal's body.

prey Animals hunted by others for food.

pterosaurs Flying reptiles that lived at the same time as dinosaurs.

spine A sharp, pointed bit of horn or bone.

stud A small, hard bit of horn or bone.

Dinosaur names

The dinosaurs and other animals in this book have long names. This is how you say them.

Allosaurus: al-oh-SAW-russ

Chirostenotes: kie-ro-sten-OH-teez

Deinonychus: dic-non-I-kuss

Dimorphodon: die-MORF-o-don

Diplodocus: di-PLOD-oh-kuss

Eoraptor: EE-oh-rap-tor

Maiasaura: my-ah-SAW-rah

Parasaurolophus: par-ah-sore-oh-loaf-us

pterosaur: TERR-oh-saw

Stegosaurus: steg-oh-SAW-russ

Tyrannosaurus rex: tie-RAN-oh-saw-russ rex

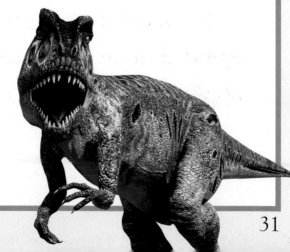

Index